A NOTE TO PARENTS ABOUT BEING CARELESS

When one could not care less about something, one is certain to be careless around it. Being careless is an expression of disrespect or disregard for something. This is why most people are often unforgiving of "accidents" that are caused by carelessness.

The purpose of this book is to teach children the importance of respecting themselves as well as the people, places, and things that surround them. It also teaches children how to translate their respect into thoughtful, careful behavior.

Reading and discussing this book with your child can help avert many of the "accidents" that bring about harm or unwanted responses from others. It can also help your child live a productive and fulfilling life that can only be attained through respect for himself or herself as well as others.

Respect is something that is "caught, not taught." Therefore, the best way to teach your child respect and carefulness is to be a person who is respectful and careful. It is to live a life in which carelessness is seldom demonstrated.

This book belongs to:

_____

Published by Scholastic Inc.
90 Old Sherman Turnpike, Danbury, CT 06816.

SCHOLASTIC and associated logos are trademarks and/or
registered trademarks of Scholastic Inc.

ISBN 0-7172-8582-0

First Scholastic Printing, October 2005

A Book About
Being
Careless

by **Joy Berry**

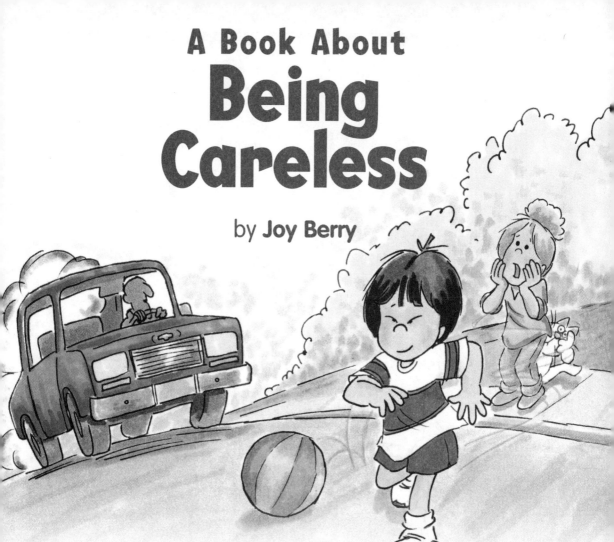

SCHOLASTIC INC.

New York   Toronto   London   Auckland   Sydney
Mexico City   New Delhi   Hong Kong   Buenos Aires

This book is about Lennie.

Reading about Lennie can help you understand and deal with **being careless.**

You are being careless when you act as if you do not care about yourself.

You are being careless when you act as if you do not care about the people and things around you.

Being careless can cause you to hurt yourself.

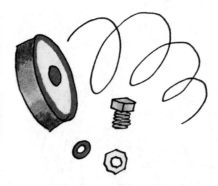

Being careless can cause you to hurt other people.

Being careless can cause you to damage or destroy things.

It is not good to be careless.

You need to *be careful* instead.

When you are careful, you act as if you care about yourself.

When you are careful, you act as if you care about the people and things around you.

Be careful.

Obey the rules.

Your parents usually know what you need to do to keep yourself and others safe. They usually know what you need to do to take care of the things around you.

The rules they make can help you be careful.

Be careful.

Pay attention to what you do so you will make fewer mistakes.

Be careful.

Slow down so you can avoid accidents and mistakes that happen when you hurry.

Be careful.

Watch where you are going so you can avoid tripping and bumping into things.

Be careful.

Be aware of people and things around you
so you can avoid dangerous situations.

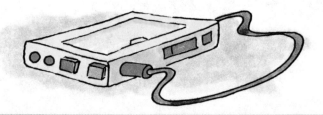

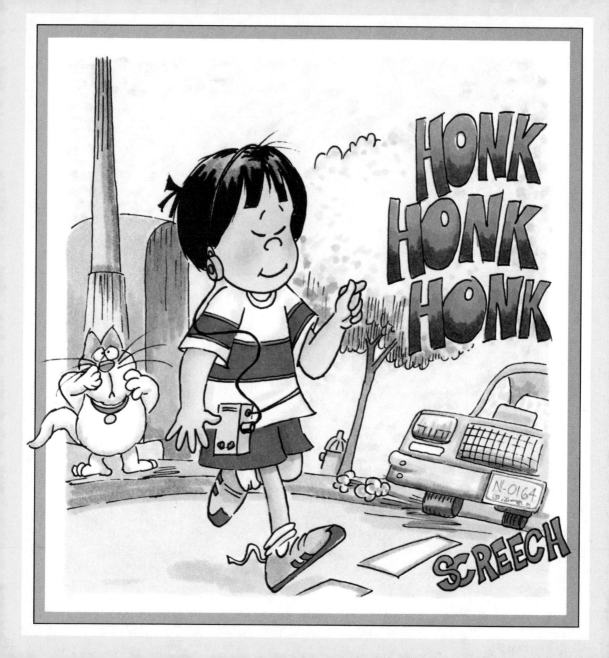

Be careful.

Avoid playing roughly so no one will get hurt and nothing will get broken.

Be careful.

Avoid playing with dangerous things so you will not hurt yourself or others.

Be careful.

Avoid playing in dangerous places so you will not hurt yourself or others.

Being careless is not good for you or the people around you.

It is better when you are careful.